MY GROANS POUR OUT LIKE WATER

Copyright © 2018
by Frances Bloom.
All rights reserved.
Printed in the United States of America.
No part of this book may be used
or reproduced in any
manner whatsoever without
written permission
except in the case of
brief quotations embodied
in critical articles or reviews.

I S B N: 978-1987460162

**My Groans
Pour Out
Like Water**

F R A N C E S   B L O O M

*This book
is dedicated
to
the memory
of
my spouse
best friend
and
childhood sweetheart*

JACOB DANTE BORAGGINA

*grief is
too weak
a word
to describe
the pain
of living
without you*

my groans

night wind **1**
where are you, Jacob? **5**
no weather **7**
companions of the wood **10**
with bated breath **14**
millennial blues **16**
church bells of avalon **19**
another day **22**
I lie here **24**
daydreams of Jacob **26**
saloon **29**
young flesh, old pains **32**
wildfire **34**
searching for something **36**
crowder mountain **40**
the bread I have will only break for you **43**
texas hill country **45**

my thoughts turn homeward 48
moonlight 50
outside of von's express 53
in dreams 55
a man I know 58
ode to the lucky ones 60
the locker room on sumner 62
the whole head is hurt 64
how can 65
september 66
my groans pour out like water 69
wake me 72
more and more 74
feet are burning 76
in ruins 78
voice of dawn 80
far west texas 82

pour out

my mother the mountain **85**
fix yourself on the southern line **89**
to those left behind **92**
a fool's blues **96**
down to the river **99**
ain't it just like this world to keep you lonesome **102**
ode to lithium **105**
freight train blues **107**
waiting around to die **109**
my friend **110**
a crack in the window **112**
what color did the moon dance? **116**
good morning blues **118**
house of mourning **120**
well shit, look at that **123**
on trinity river **126**
first manic episode **128**

wounded soldier **131**
ode to a fluted dawn **134**
state fairgrounds **136**
a quick poem before my psychotherapy appointment **141**
a rhythm to the struggle **145**
a widow's whisper
(and I ain't talkin' about the california kind) **149**
fixin' to die **150**
when I fall into dreaming **152**
junkie blues **156**
gold in my pocket **159**
I love the smoker **162**
death is not stronger than love **167**
I am going to rise this morning **170**
road to nowhere **171**
the call of the barn swallow **173**
ode to weltschmerz **175**

like water

the craftsman that carves **178**
my love **179**
lost on metropole avenue **185**
wild water **188**
the lamb is worthy **191**
on faith **194**
I tried to live for a rose pogonia **196**
walk across the plains **200**
along the railroad **205**
pecan creek **209**
go to war **211**
golden night **214**
I really want to know **217**
loony bin love song **222**
me and the devil **225**
southern train got my lungs **230**
dirtbag charmer **233**

the morning sun **235**
blackbird blues **237**
everything is just about the same **239**
sprinkle me **241**
I will be **243**
midnight glitter **245**
waste of space **247**
be careful **249**
when you are broken, the gifts keep coming **251**
rider on a white horse **253**
the sky is not glowing **255**
pumped dry **256**

NIGHT WIND

my love
rides in
on a night wind,
he battles the
steepest hills
and crumbles
with the morning ash-
and while I long
for days
gone by
he shines me
with a wink.

my love
lights the candles
like a wild horse
sparks a flame
on the heels
of a crimson dusk.

my love
speaks with
bottled sunshine
and lies awash
with a spirited tempo.

my love
bakes
and
sculpts
my lips
as he salts

my wounds
and shapes perfume
into butter.

my love
blows me a kiss
more wild
than
the fog
layering
the lowlands.

my love
touches me
with a tingle
as he floats
steady
above a
warm sea.

my love
always finds me
when I am wading
shoulder deep
in the rapid currents,

but my love
could not save me
from the
miles
and
miles

of grasslands
with no
footsteps
on the dirt,

he could not
warn me
about the flocks
of the careless
hiding out
in a
fair-weather
june tide,

he could not
prepare me
for
the droves
of sorrow
or the rope
that
would soon
tie me
down
to these
iron trails.

my love-
are you drinking
from the sweet
waters of the
far north,

or are you
on the path
of an old drive
with a great herd
by your side?

as I wonder
where you are,
I am more
lonesome
than
the coyote
howling
at the
scattered milk
dripping from
the night sky-

stay with me
sweet raven,
just until the
red flutter
at dawn
makes
the flakes
of sun
turn blue.

WHERE ARE YOU, JACOB?

the fields
of sky
drip far and wide
and make way for
a clear
desert morning.

I find myself
looking deep
into the soft dawn
because I know
just as the sun rides
over these mountains,
the citrus swirl
of the early hours
can make
the blues at my feet
stay quiet,

if just for a breath.

the milky arms
of the saguaro
are standing
taller than me,

this salted path
and grain lit wind
got ahold of my shoes
and
beats down
my collapsing lungs.

my heart
soars
far,
far
away.

and
even though
I am above
the snakes
with kerosene
on my hands,
even though
I am drinking
applejack
while
barking
at a knot,
this place
and the truck
that got me here
might be
one of the
loneliest moments
a fool like me,
takes home.

where are you, Jacob?

NO WEATHER

I once told myself
the winter sure did
walk beside me.

I once told myself
the fleshy haze
of springtime
and the
barefoot glow
of summer
would never find
my back door,
but I know better now-

I am in the land of no weather.

the windless rain
could be drying my lips
and the slippery roads
could be melting my feet
but my steps
still fall
under the patchy fog
into
the valley
of the unknown.

like the hunted
waking up to the day,
I am out of place
with no disguise.

the floods here
are without flow
and the heat
cannot break
into the distant
easterly winds.
hard snow
cannot be found
when
blue frost
melts
into coal.

there are no
rolls of thunder
or late morning rains
to deliver memories
of your carefree childhood,
whole
as it was
entire.

only in the land of no weather
do you smell
the violence
of a sagging sky
and
the calls of
a wistful chest,
touching some
woolen
burning skin.

I am in the land of no weather,

it is a high climbing
type of gloom
that carries big guns
but finds itself
tangled in the clouds.

no one flees from
the sun here
because
every drop
tastes about the same.
the day and night
might as well be
left and right,
and your cottony dreams?
well,
they are better off
making
bitter swells
to scratch up
by
the dawn.

COMPANIONS OF THE WOOD

companions
of the wood
and
settlers
of the night sky,
those who light fires
in the canyon halls
and those who dream
of a burning meadow,
who among you
can walk beside me
and tell me a sweet tale?

distract my mind,
more than
the salt I am swallowing
the broth I am smelling
the chords I am strumming
the highways I am driving
or
the honey I am stirring.

walk with me
after the storm
and
well beyond
the clouds.
tell me to stop
because I am slipping.

this living stuff,
well shit

it has pushed me
down a slope.

I am laying on
a wooden board
shaking in a cold sweat.

my engine
is breaking
and
the journey
is just,
god awful.

I am
without direction
as my toes
lean into my lungs,
for high above
the clapping hands
I am at
the beginning
of the
fastest sport
on ice.

but I am not driving this sled.

I might have a crowd
cheering me on
but
their love

is not strong enough
to mount me
on the ground.

so,
to those
who have mercy
on a young drunk
with racing thoughts
and inside voices at work,
tell me a story
or
mail me a letter
full of distractions,
not because you want
something
from me
but because
you want to give me-
muttering hope
scalding love
or maybe
just another
clotted breath.

tell me the story
you spell out to your cousins,
the secrets
only your sister knows,
tell me all the
moments
of mystery.

let me taste
the plastic
on your lips
and the faith
in your
eyelids,

walk with me on
this lonesome street
and be my
companion of the wood.

WITH BATED BREATH

with bated breath,
my throat is burned.
with malted hands,
my thumbs unfold.
with crooked ears,
my tears thicken.

weary eyes,
please.
before my sun goes setting
and while the day
is still hanging high-

send me the darkness
ahead of the drought.
send me the yoke
ahead of the chains.
send me the seed
ahead of the vine.

turn your back
on those who
break often
and enter slowly,
for on these smoking hills
I have made
my strength
his flesh.

his wounds are mine
and my clothes
carry the sounds

of my crying lips
falling on footsteps
forced to walk
without
the shady grove
I was promised,
the one
stolen
by
the breath
of fate itself.

have you covered yourself with a cloud?
is no prayer getting through?
there is no compassion
in these welts
you have left
on my arms
and
in my lungs.

I am scattered,
like pieces of stone
on a temple street.

MILLENNIAL BLUES

the audible events
of the day
and pictures from
around the world,
give noisy
amusement
to the hungry children
who fold their thumbs
with all the
determination
and prowess
of their grandmothers,
molding
swirls
of
cinnamon
from rejected
pieces
of
pie crust.

there is something baking here,

my brothers
and sisters
are told
to keep
swiping
and
pressing.

scroll until

you need
to soap up your skin,
twist your nails
until they
bleed out
something
tepid
and
stifled.

not one minute
can those hands
be idle
because
you know what they say,
idle hands are the devil's workshop.

check-in
tell us where you are
tell us where you have been
post
and comment
and post
and then,

oh-
you will lose that frill.
life will make you weep.

I remember
when I lost it
too.

you got
blood in your eyes
kid
and because
you never learned
how to
sit with suffering
or hell,
even sit and read…

my friends,
in all those years
of posing
and
shedding
you have been smothered
away from
the thing
you are
terrified of
but
the
only thing
that can set you free-

yourself.

CHURCH BELLS OF AVALON

what is
chewing at
my troubled mind?
I can feel
squirming legs
wheezing behind
my dripping eyes
as the winter chill
pours
down
the throat
of these syrupy hills.

I am bonded
with the church bells
of avalon
in grief.
oh yes,
these bells
grieve with me
as they
summon
my footsteps
on a busy street.

my reply
drains out
a pair of
sweating lungs
and a
moldy heart.

their melody
blows on
the back of
a northern wind.
they whisper through
the window
and can be heard
haunting the old woods,
reminding the dusk
to turn down the day.

I hoped they could
bring me ease
on this
miserable
island.
an impossible task,
even for the bells
shaped out of
filtered dreams.

but there is
something
to see
and
something
to hear
with every clink
that passes by
these bells,
with every note
that presses

on the sun
and hums
the gloomy
strings
of midnight.

and
even though
no footsteps
rhyme with mine,
down
the old
chime tower
road
you are never
really
never,
alone.

ANOTHER DAY

today
is just like all the rest,
each noonday sun
has blended
with the last.
some more lonesome
than others,
but none of this shit is living.

the sky has swept
away from the clouds,
and the stagnant meat
oozes with the frost
of a sprinkled night.

there is no splendid disguise
for this kind of pain-
every breath is soaked
in your loss.
there is no spellbinding tide
or far-reaching stone.
no drinking
from their eyes.
it is just
endless sorrow.

goddammit this hurts-

laying with the torture
of the abundant murk
like some fading sea,

my eyes
steam up
like a creamy
morning mist.

my mind
feels like honey
bursting from its comb.

my heart
has grown wrinkled
from hours
in
the river.

and some nights
as the wind swells in,
I think my grief
could make
the day
stand still.

I LIE HERE

as water wears away stones,
I lie here.

as night swallows the day,
I lie here.

as our books,
once resting in the sweet air
gather dust
I lie here.

as your clothes lay gently in boxes,
mourning the loss of their master's body
I lie here.

as wind gives the arms
of your favorite trees
direction,
I lie here.

as smoke layers above the sea,
I lie here.

as your ashes sit on our table,
I lie here.

I lie here
bathing in sorrow
forsaken,
and
unable
to swallow my fate.

I lie here
unable to build,
without strength to tear down.

I lie here
unable to keep
and
unable to throw away.

I lie here
not wishing I were dead
not wishing I were alive
but wishing I had never existed,
for then I would never know
the suffering
that settles
under the sun.

DAYDREAMS OF JACOB

a gently washed
string quartet
powdered with
a choir
of wild poppy,
rests empty and barren
when matched
to the sound
of his voice.

the slope
on the ocean floor
and the depth
of underwater islands,
seem to fade quickly
from imagination
when reminded
of
the warm
chocolate
in his eyes.

a cluster
of sand grains,
bounded by
mountain ranges
lose their matrimony,
when I think of our
naked bodies
lying side by side.

the smell

of toasted minerals
on a river
lined with clay
falls west to the breeze
when I am caught
daydreaming
of the blossom glaze
on his lips,
as they lifted
to the sky.

the drifters stop flameworking
and the artifacts remain
salted in dust
when the curious
men and women
finally, see what I see-
the poetry
in his skin
and
the wild rose
pumping from
his heart.

many have attempted
to follow his footsteps
in desperation and in trial,
but they could never
breathe in
the smoke
that pours out
from the rushing water-

like a butter knife
sliced into the earth
and hidden inside
was victoria falls.

and just like the way
the devil fights
the archangel
in the dawn
of the north-
and just like the way
the andean flamingos
walk among the
clouded flats-
no matter how hard you try
none of these things
could ever be replicated,

like the spirit of my Jacob
like the sound of his voice
like the touch of his raven hair
falling on sweet skin,
like a
creamy
purple
columbine
throwing petals
to the wind.

SALOON

there is a saloon
for record keeping
due east of the land,
where stars come out to play.

everyone is thirsty
for the giggle water here.

tourists walk in
carrying the taste
of spring on their lips
but quickly dust out,
which is good for us
because those people
beat their gums
all
day
long.

this place
hides the flesh
of the saddened,
it is a resting spot
for those burning
with the blue flame.

there is no apple butter here.
no exchanging
stories of recent trips
to south america
or carrying on about
nonprofit work that

was featured
in some well-read blog.
there are no eyebrow raises
or disapproving glances
over ignorance of
a local zine
or a new band
that protests lyrics.

there is none of that
mutual mediocrity
that people my age
seem to eat up.

here,
you can smell
the rattling of the cages
and
feel the threads
when they stick out.

and those of us
gathered here
with poor posture
and dirty hands,
praise a good storyteller
with a
well delivered
punchline.

we tingle for
the moment

we are in
because
so often
we escape
the straight way back,
tuning out
the heart
with a frosted sip.

YOUNG FLESH, OLD PAINS

I have young flesh
all marked up
with old pains.
and while the sideways clock
shuts down the wind,
we are left here
to meet in the morning-
as noah's dove once whispered,
life ain't worth living
without the one you love.

but there is something
in the doing
that is needed
for the why.

the song
I am singing
comes in
on a whistling trill,
and is older than
the exodus bell
itself.

when I see their skin
that looks like mine
I have to stoop down
so I don't bump my head.
I have to hang tight
so I don't drop my luggage.
I have to cool the flames
so I don't distill the wash.

I have to fly downriver
so I don't sink my core.
I have to worship
the dry giant,
so I don't scrape
my running feet.

but no matter how
I struggle and stride,
I always
have to
jump the line.
I always come back,
roaring under
the night sky.

I never find myself in these people,

it must be
my young flesh
all marked up
with old pains.

WILDFIRE

the days are coming in
just like smoke
riding with
the wind,
in a matter of minutes
the golden grass
and wired rods
will turn
black.

I am in the line of fire
and each morning
is proof
of a narrow escape.
the smell of forest cinder
will hang heavy
while the understory crackle
exhales
and
nails
the soles of my feet.

meadow animals flee,
leaping with their fur ablaze
as trees hold steady
to the northern edge
of the woods-
nature has taken the living
and crumbled it into ash.
wildfires cremate
all the still life
that swayed

and
glittered
in yesterday's moonlight.

maybe this is why
so many
fear the distant sight
of a smoldering sky.

sure,
there is an element of danger-
the heat of the flames,
canyon smoke,
and months of drought
could make
fast fuel
for the appetite
of the blanketing sun.
but maybe
the hunger of the fire
is just too violent
to bare.
the smell of the night
too lonely
to cope with.
a mark of a
predestined truth,
that the
midnight snow
remembers

in time, we all will burn.

SEARCHING FOR SOMETHING

there is a ghost town here,
a place to find
not myself
but my past self.
a place to hear the dead
and bond
in our
shared sorrows.

maverick mountain
lies to the east
and the crumble
of the dry soil
hitting the rocks
stuck to my feet
is as lyric as the
shadowy skies
of dawn.

the river here
falls from
the rockies
and
bends the
desert footsteps
of texas,
while the
crippled shrubs
make their home
underneath
the rugged arms
of pine canyon.

big bend country is my home.

I wish I could be an outlaw
and escape across this river,

"well, ma'am she has fled to another country
by way of the rio grande"

but it never works when
your enemy
is yourself
and what
you are
running from
never leaves your side.

so it looks like I am
bound for something,
between these
shining rocks
and
miles of
light
that ribbons down
beside the
cliffs.

I used to clean myself
in these waters
but now it takes
a heavy dose of booze
to forget that I need cleaning,

to forget about the
mess I have in front of me
and all the goodness left behind.

this landscape enchanted me,
it enchanted us-
we loved
to love
under
the clear skies of dark.
we used to talk about
the music of this place
and the rambling in the air,

but doing this without you?

oh man-

just like the way
all this desert
once was
under the sea,

it is something
I cannot
make sense of
and never will.

but I still
find myself
back here,
drinking whiskey

by the mountain sage
and howling
with the winter winds
and I guess,

searching for something.

CROWDER MOUNTAIN

this night is
cornering me
even though
I ain't bothering no one.
I cannot be fed
in the darkness
of this day.

under the
bitter rains
of crowder mountain,
I feel leaves
weeping on my shoulder
and needles
coating the breeze.

a father
and daughter
share a memory
soon to be forgotten,
they find themselves
fully in these woods.
and me?
I am gritting my teeth

aghhhhhhhhhhhhh-

how can people do this?
you see,
I can drink
and deliver
a genuine laugh,

I can wear his ripped socks
and my dirty clothes,
but still
feel like
a complete stranger
to myself.

my lonesome fiddle
sheds its tune
alongside
the weighted waters
and rutted shores.
but when the night comes on,
I am left with
the silence
of a falling star.

shit,
look
at the way
the night
is coming down-

there is famine in my soul.
there is thirst in my heart.
I am staggering
from
sea
to
coast,

I am crawling

from
south
to
west,

I am
lying
in hours
of guilt
and
weeks
of
shame.

I am melted
in
grief
and
dwelling
in mourn,

and the truth is,
I could die right here
along this corridor trail
with pathway stones
at my feet,
and feel like
the blessed
have delivered me
something holy.

THE BREAD I HAVE WILL ONLY BREAK FOR YOU

the day hits westward
and melts the wind
over rusted steel
while sifting
sunlight
into porches
around noon.

echoes of lovers
and whispers of sons
soon to be lost by time,
gently rush by-
I am all but whole
but this I know,
the bread I have will only break for you.

no matter
the stations I roam
the valleys I creep
or the highways I park,
there will always be
a car full of the restless
eager to take my money
and turn it into ears on the floor.

there will be a time
when life crushes you down.
we will all stand before
the drifting moonlight,
fighting like warriors
with our fate in hand
and lying still,

collapsed
by the weight
of frosted nails.

our son was never born
but I can hear
his laugh
in the sharp air.

his father is not here,
he is just a memory.
his tender eyes-
shaped like almonds
and soft like buttercream
are now
the ash from flames.

but lying still
among the lonely
and drinking
with the poor,
I could never love another
how I love our family
because
I am only sure
of just one thing,

the bread I have will only break for you.

TEXAS HILL COUNTRY

sitting on a lonesome rock,
looking out at
miles and miles
of hills,
the desert spoon
is somewhere close
I can feel it
as my hands
fall flat
with the tumble.

silver wire
shapes the road
and I can see
a yellow house
up on the ridge,
out here
in texas hill country.

this is the first
I have smelled
the sun
in two weeks.
I have been melting
under the motel sheets
drinking white whiskey,
dreaming about the ghosts
of spanish monks,
and holding my beloved
far too close.

far too close,

that the morning light
makes my spit turn sour.
I slouched down
on the plastic chair
beside my door,
and looked around.
the wind blew crisper
than usual
and the moss was
hanging thick.
thick enough
to hide the
abandoned metal,
baking out here
in the noon's black mud.

I thought I would stand up
say hello to the world,
walk with these
sorrowed trails
and forgotten wildflowers-
talk to you out loud.
fool myself,
thinking you are alive.

to my surprise
I met a friend.
he was only nine,
but he reminded me of you.
he was throwing rocks
against these limestone walls,
and splitting them open.

he told me,
put your arm in it, girl!

when his father called him
I began to weep.
he made me feel so close to you
and just for a breath,
I thought I could stick it out.
I fell to my feet
as the truck drove away

and there I was,
sitting on a lonesome rock
looking out at
miles and miles
of hills,
the desert spoon
is somewhere close
I can feel it
as my hands
fall flat
with the tumble.

MY THOUGHTS TURN HOMEWARD

the road from huntsville
is a long and winding one.
the tennessee river
runs and mourns,
its water shimmers
like oil in the face
of the sun.

you can find me
down by
the sipsey fork,
I am out here
trying to find grace-
but just like looking for
rainbow trout
in these waters,
it don't come easy.

I have lost my will to live

but maybe I can
find it here
in these foothills,
if the black crow
can fly with the blues
surely I can.

but each breath comes out on fire,
like jet fuel
trailing over the sky,
I can track my sorrows
as they burn.

I want to be free.
I want to overcome this.
I want to lean into
the winding stream
and see compassion.
I want to find goodness
and godliness
in all beings,
even myself.

but down here,
by the sipsey fork-
time is running out.
in the fields
and farmlands of
south tuscaloosa county,
I am holding onto
the crying song
of the cliff swallows.

I am praying
to be as as free
as these swamp streams.
I have to find a way
back home in here.
I want these woods to be
a lighted candle
my lighted candle,
and keep
my prayers alive
in the southern winds
of home.

MOONLIGHT

there is no light
that wanders
with me,
under these western stars.

there is no smile
that tames me
beside strangers walking
feet
by
foot.

there is no sound that dulls me
there is no liquid that numbs me
there is no fire that molds me
there is no tile that cools me.

under the mellow lamp
of the twinkling sea,
there is little to admire
because my body is crumbling.

pathways auction themselves,
but no one finds me.
my breath is moving
and spitting with the wind
but inside,
there is a force
that prays to quit.

holy hands
resting on

my knees
tell me
time is only
but a verdict.

when the trees
lie motionless
and clover
begins to wilt,

when winter
shades out
all my spring,

when fair skin
bruises at the touch,

when dry storms
pace alongside me,

well,
I guess that means
my days
are numbered.

the moonlight
that is falling,
and
the silver shimmer
that hangs freely
in the midnight glaze,
has not

found me
in quite some time.
but soon,
I will become that light.

I will enchant
young lovers
and
my restless glitter
will smile down,
filling
the night
with everything
I could not
give
to the day.

OUTSIDE OF VON'S EXPRESS

take my hands
fill them with water.
take my eyes
clean them with daydreams.
take my lips
feed them with silence.

I awoke in these
dripping hours
to the summer song
of the cicadas.
no one told me
it would be like this,
I found twenty-seven links
of chain around my feet.
I tried to speak
but no words came out,

people pass by but offer no help.

please do this for me-
just one thing I ask.
dig me down low
near some hillside river
with crimson leaves
spread along a pebbly bank.
keep my gold chain
loose around my neck.

lay me with his
ashes in my hands.
tell the wandering guests that

the sun did peep through,
but only when
we were together.
throw yellow flowers
near our bodies
and sing a song
we once loved.

unlike my love
sprinkled on me,
I will not die
with my boots on.
you can tell them
to take
all that is left,
just leave me here
with him.

death will surely
save me
from mourning
my young life away
with
years of sleep
and
high wine.

IN DREAMS

wake me,
chirping birds
dawn skies,
warm me-
blow sun into the
skins of my eyes.
dripping paint,
fold me
shaking pipes,
silence me.

there is a
faint sound
of strings,
must be the kitchen television.
these lonesome sonatas
drip
like a milk fever
from an artist
lost and tilled.

but this morning
I woke up with a smile.
I soaked up a moment of peace.

I went searching in my mind,
why do I feel this way?

oh yes,
I found it.

I was with Jacob last night.

I kissed him.
I felt his soft
knitted cheeks.
I held his hand.
I told him,
I love your voice.

I was finally given
what my knees
have been
praying for,
more time-

just a second more.

I saw his eyes smile
with young caramel skin.
I got drunk on the flames
of his
holy lips.

he is back!
he must be in the kitchen
making us breakfast
or down the street
grabbing me coffee
or,

aghhhhhhhhhhhhhh.

my waking eyes
slowly bring into focus

the blurred shapes
around me.

I am far away from that life
with no trace of
him
me
or
us.

how cruel
in this,
the dawns hour.
and I sink
into the sheets
weeping
at the sounds
of the day
walking in.

A MAN I KNOW

there is a man I know
who walks around
with iron strings
laced through his fist,
decorated
in a floral shirt
and old brown jeans.

the rubber on his shoes
has gone smooth,
balding from
all the hours
walked in this place.
his teeth are few
and his shining
silver mouth
greets me
as noon hovers
above the trees.

this man does not
ask for much-
no raise.
no work gloves.
not even a door
left open
for his busy hands
and quiet mind.

he runs this museum.
he hangs
the very frames

those wealthy tourists
examine and admire.
he builds the
life-size versions
of whimsically illustrated
board games,
he dusts the antique island pottery,
he sweeps the halls
and snakes the drains,
he shovels shit,
he runs this place.

and you my brother,
are seen and heard
by almost no one.
but
I see you,
and I think what you do
is more worthy of praise
than all the forgotten faces
that adorn these walls.

I see you,
and I think what you do
is more worthy of praise,
than whatever
these fools do
that keeps them paying
17 dollars for admission.

ODE TO THE LUCKY ONES

my mind needs no permission to wander,
my heartbeat needs no taming,
the city smells
need no covering,
and the fisherman
needs no calming
because
tomorrow has not begun
and it may never begin
for the stooped aged grocer
with wispy gray hairs,
skin hanging loose
beside her cloudy eyes.
for the middle-aged man
with leather baked hands,
trying to make a fresh start.

the skies of tomorrow
and the soft glow
of morning
may never
soak the flesh
of the sad wandering child,
too fat to be loved
of the heroin addict,
trying to silence
the voices in his mind
of the generation kid,
desperate to be liked by all
even herself,
of the doctors
who know my song

but refuse to sing it,
of those who ride
the wings
of summer
on this island
buying memories for no one-
drinking themselves
instead of
knowing themselves,
of people who may never
gain the wisdom
of how endless
this all can be

and man,
aren't they the lucky ones?

THE LOCKER ROOM ON SUMNER

I am a
desperate
lonely
drunk
who knows
this feeling
all too well,
the fire of longing
when I shake my head.

only a
desperate
lonely
drunk
can hear whispers
from the chairs
as minutes melt into days,
as my mind folds into butter,

praying for
a rising tide
or
a midnight fog
to hang low.

no,
you ain't the only one
to feel rotten
but I was
the only one
that
breathed in

his hair
every
morning.
I was the only one
that licked his skin
every
evening.

please,
lord
fool me.
no one better tell me
that in this
january wind
he is just
another part
of the
forgotten dead.

THE WHOLE HEAD IS HURT

the whole head
is hurt
and
the whole heart
is sick,
from the soles
of my feet
to
the top of my head,
every spot is injured.
my soul
ain't
soothed with oil-
it is
bubbling
with
sores.

I am so alone.

HOW CAN

how can the wind
dance
at my window,
when I lie
in
pieces
with the
night?

how can the birds
praise the
morning fog,
when
my chuck
pours out
like sap?

how can my
neighbors sing
of roses,
when my
hands
have been
chiseled
down-
soaking wrists
is all
I got
left.

how can this all be?

SEPTEMBER

I wish
the earth shook
quaked
and trembled
in the cold
undisturbed hours
of that morning.

I wish
smoke engulfed the sky,
darkening the city streets.
I wish fire
illumined the hills-
collapsing
anything
green
flowering
or
floating
in the gentle meadows.

I wish
for the wind to cease
and for beautiful sounds
like,
piano sonata no.2 in b-flat minor, op. 35
to fall on deafened ears.

I wish for an eternal night,
and a hopeless winter
to settle my torn flesh.

I wish commercials would
stop worshiping
the folly of you people-
the ones who never mourn.

I wish the birds to quiet
grasshoppers to
lose their delight
and
for children to weep.

but none of this came true
the morning after
I held your hand
and kissed
the freckle behind
your left ear
for the last time.

none of this came true
the morning after
I came home
to your body,
motionless
and bent
beside our
favorite window.

none of this came true
the morning after
I kissed the blue
corners of your face.

none of this came true
the morning after
I whispered-
every part of you
has always been
as holy
as the wind in my hand
as the water beneath my feet
as the midnight stones
in the sky.

but none of this came true,

and I cannot
look strangers in the eye.
I cannot smile
without aches in my teeth.

life has kept moving,
and the rivers of sorrow
that carve
through the
canyons in my bones
are invisible to all.

even you.

MY GROANS POUR OUT LIKE WATER

job-
my brother.
I know of
your suffering
as you curse
the burning sea
and
slacking tides.
I am powerless
with you
in my grief,
but your sighing words
feel like home
to my
bleeding gums
and
battered soul.

I too ask,
why take him from the world?
why leave me here?
why not deliver me to the grave?

I am hopelessly tangled
with smoke at my breath
and fire under my feet.

please
I beg of you-
do not show me
the breaking of dawn,
another lightless day

moving forward
but without sound,
like a spinning disc
torn up with scratches
these days
pour out
with few words
and
even less
meaning.

yes
my groans pour out like water,
just like you said they would.

but job-
my brother.
I do not wish
to rest beside kings,
trapped with men
that roam drunk
on their
own status.

I do not wish
to be in the company
of those
sleeping in linen,
the mighty queens
adorned in the
gold fabrics
of a wasted life.

I only wish to rest,
to be free
of all this living.
no more reaching
for the touch
of his hands,
no more kissing
the dimpled cheeks
on our unborn children
upon
every
waking
hour.

job-
my brother.
how did you make
it through the loss
and the sightless sounds
of all these
miserable
comforters?

I do not wish to be saved.

I just want
to smolder these
tortured mornings-
figure out
how to burn up
their low-down ways
and even deeper spells.

WAKE ME

wake me,
but only if
his golden tongue is here,
climbing like a rose
turning solid into crystal.

wake me,
but only if his fingers
wet my skin
delicate as a
flat leaved orchid
with fruit so pure,
the scent of spicewood
hangs heavy
on his lips.

wake me,
but only if
his voice
will guide me
like the greater honey bird
that leads
my sisters and brothers
to find bees in the wild-
take me to the
sweet taste
of his voice.

wake me,
but only if you can
bend my dreams
and shape them from gas,

make them clay
and bring him back
from the dust.

wake me,
but only if my mind
stays quiet
and my heart
breathes still.

oh,
cruel morning
I am still resting
from a cruel night
do not wake me
just to smother
me in the bark
of curdled figs.

day
after
day
what you see
on the bed here,
this is darkness.
this is fading.
this is sorrow.

this is grief.

MORE AND MORE

I am looking for
something
stronger than
barrel char
more sedating
than swill
more
and
more
and
more.

I am on the hunt
for some
blowing flame
that keeps me
sleeping
through the day
and singing
with the night,
something with
more catch
than a ragtime waltz.

hit me with the good stuff
because
I need more blues
for my tapping feet
and rambling mind,
I need more stank
than all those
smokestacks

resting
on the tidelands.

I need warm salt
thicker than pulp
and
juicing down
my rotted breath.

I want to feel numb
without swallowing.
I want euphoria
without
masturbating,
shooting up,
or
sucking down.

I am looking for
something
stronger than
barrel char
more sedating
than swill
more
and
more
and
more.

FEET ARE BURNING

my days are spent
like the
flattened stones
near the bottom
of a narrow canyon
steeper than
it is wide,
all covered
in midnight
even at noon.

the skin on my feet
has turned into char.
no hill
could hide
my sorrow.
the tallest of peaks
could never
shade out
my grief.
no land can heal me.
no light can shine me.

I am a restless soul,
not waiting
around to find
meaning
but very caught up
in the end,
a slow crawl
some might say.

when morning
falls behind me
and my breath
chokes on grit,
I can recognize
this familiar feeling-
six hours
without
that
sweet whiskey
on my lips.

rest your head easy for a while,
he whispers
I am right here.

but you ain't.
I am talking to the wind,
praying the words on a sign
or the hollow static
of the radio
is a message from the dead.

but it ain't.
it is just me out here,
drunk
lonely
and
sick,
counting every beat
with a sigh.

IN RUINS

crumbling ruins
seem to chase
rolling cliffs
from
this world
to the next,
but I was
always taught
a breaking wave
lands just
before the
coast.

is death
a meadow of grass,
growing fast
and
flowering freely
after a long
hard
burn?

or
are the
glistening
summer skies
and pastel clouds
something to
smell in
just this skin?

are we to only thrive

on this mashed-up land
clinging to a deep sea,
or will we
say hello to our
mothers and fathers,
shot
abandoned
and
dispossessed?

I have no answers
for me
and either do you,
but when I
walk the hilltops
and swim across
these untamed rivers,
when I breathe in
the dusty old west
and ride along
the iron trails
at dawn,

I feel
this may be it
and
I bow
my head
in sorrow.

VOICE OF DAWN

voice of dawn
bring me strength
today,
help me love myself
or
at least
be kind to myself.

voice of dawn
ship my troubles
down the red hills,
send me
his voice
his feet
his warmth
and
his smile.

these tears,
the ones
ripping lines
down my cheeks-
help me turn
them into
morning dew
or
sun and shadow.

voice of dawn
look at my soul,
it has been
trampled

by moose
in a shy woodland.
feel my skin,
like wet metal
gone rusted.

patch up my heart,
it is ripping
like some
cheap cloth
chasing out the wind.
just make me something else,
give me form
like the way
the river
gently scrapes
up the floor.
grant my hands
rope for my mind
or at least
buy me a little mercy.

voice of dawn
send me a reason
why
I should
even reason
and
maybe then,
I can hold onto
another day.

FAR WEST TEXAS

those far west texas
clouds,
they sure are
coming in quick
like a tide
climbing up the sand
and pouring over
the trans-pecos,
is this what makes
my next breath
worth breathing?

ah,
the whistle of the wind-
no getting enough of it.
the hours keep
passing through
as I rest
above the mist.

I find myself
just south of alpine,
I drove beyond
the fog layer
and from up here
I can see
the whites
of the sky
hanging low.

there is
warmth

up here
and that sound,
the whistle of the wind-
it has
my eyes
well watered
and
my tongue
peeling off
the skin
hanging from
my lips

I drink in the cold,
my mind is pacing
but my body
keeps still
and I think
these bighorn sheep
are making silence
with
the meadows.

the clouds spill
so clean,
they seem almost
built
to
spill.

and
the song

this place
got humming
is fragile
to the touch
but sitting right
below my feet.

I must be
seeing the light
from some holy ground,
like when
we would
jump
into an
icy spring
and gaze
at the sun
underneath
the
rippled
water.

this sacred wind takes me in-

and lucky for me,
I am
breathing filthy
and
muttering
desperate enough
to hear
its sounds.

MY MOTHER THE MOUNTAIN

salted grain,
lace my fingers
burning stars,
drip me cold
tameless sky,
paddle through me
north wind,
find me
and
dance me
in rags.
cut my silk
into string
and
keep me
circling
around the drain.

my mother's hands
lie before me.
her dark eyes
mesmerize all,
all
but the
guadalupe mountains.

wandering beside
waterless paths
and
pointed flesh,
I smile at
the face

of fate itself,
the mercy
of our creator
perhaps.
these mountains
once under water
finally,
stand
tall enough
to see the sun-
puffed up
and taking
a breath
after so
many years
buried
in the dark,

they found home.

my time left here
is spent waiting
for death
or
dreaming of it,
a double fold
kind of living.

but there
sure is
something
so beautiful

about those
who set themselves free.
just like these mountains,
even just the sight
of the mighty
el capitan,
can help the lonesome
like me
breathe easy
for a while.

a halfway point for the soul,
like how it was
for those
who rode
the
old stagecoach line
from memphis to
san francisco-
you can turn back here
or
keep heading west.

oh lord,

just the sight
of that
flat-topped peak
dancing
high above
desert flowers
can make

a worried rambler
fold some
fleeting light
into their pocket,
and sometimes
that is
all
you
got.

FIX YOURSELF ON THE SOUTHERN LINE

coming down the bend
there is a train
whistling away
the blues,
here she goes-
taking me down
that mighty
long road.

I can hear the
squeaking songs
of night
as snow
from the
white hills
covers all
but
those
metal rails.

one must have
a worried mind
and a troubled heart
to ride the blues out
on this line,
and the fine men
and women aboard
have nothing to do
and all day to do it.

you will find
many things on this path-

collapsed rails
and broken bridges,
cattle will get lost on the tracks
and boilers might catch fire,
crossties will go rotten
and
because
we are powered
by the pines
of the
southland,
we are bound to stop
and cut us down
some more fuel.
sparks from
the wood fires
might just take you
but worry not,
you are about
to go down with the flames
and help power
this smoking cannonball.
the flares are
coming for you
like clotted milk
hidden in a malt,
but soon you will
ride along
the tilting rocks
and flowing lowlands.
you can rest easy
and glint across

the mighty mississippi.

if the blues follow you
with every breath,
there is only
one place to go
and
only you
can find that ticket.

it will come to you
on a cloudy day
when the rain is
slicing down
but the
sunlight
is
peeking
through,

trying to make up
for all that
lost time
I suppose.

TO THOSE LEFT BEHIND

I am sorry
for my weak
and pathetic self.
please forgive me-

you might think
I am in the middle
of a mighty tempest,
the cold wind
and teething hail
bound to let up
before
I light a shuck.

you might think
the warm shores
will appear
and
the hills will
rise above
all this
flooded marsh,

but as the day gets darker
and the night makes
a fool out of me
I must tell you
my dying wish,

do not mourn
the rest of your years
for me.

take some time
to wet your eyes as you
sink my skin
with a
half-whispered
prayer.

I am without pain now.
I am
back in the arms
of my love
or
I have fallen
to the dark night

lights off–

but both
are better than
treading in
the shallows
with echoes
of voices
in my hands
and around
my neck.

for you,
my mother–
there is
a yellow moon
on the way

you will see the
grass falling
under the stockade.
there will be
a stillness
and a call
of the seabirds
begging for dawn.

and you will
find me in their love,

you will always find me.

do not let
the candlelight
beat you down.

do not let the
twilight mock you.

do not become water
out to sea.

please,
do not follow me.

stay afloat,
fight what your eyes
are selling you,
rest beside one another,
breathe in the icy air,

sigh out
the warmth of my light,
and
above all else
stay close
to the turning
of the day.

A FOOL'S BLUES

I am a fool
for thinking
something
you could say
or do
would relieve
an ounce
of my pain.

I am a fool
for thinking I can send
my starless nights
into the mind of another
or the eyes
of a stranger.

there are melting stones
at my ankles
and a stirring river
under my hands,

like planting corn
on a moonless night
this oat patch
thrives in my breath
and sweats out
my blood.

I am a fool
for thinking
any kind of cloud
could ever save me

from the loneliness
of your loss,
like miles
drifting slowly
across
the hard tablelands.

the well flowered
shorelines
cannot save me
because I am separated
from other people,
now more than ever

like a spoiled
stretch of forest
or a rambling river
in the rugged west,
I am all cut tangled
to the souls beside me.

I want to find
myself with you.
I want to escape
the caves of man
and the
barefoot paths
of solitude,
but my sweet love
has died in my hands
and the cold water
found in the fields

of all this living
will never leave my side.
I just hope
to become
a casual passerby-
to swirl back
into the heart
of a dreamer,
to distill some
of this aching,
and to toss
the battered
parts
of myself
into the fire.

DOWN TO THE RIVER

I took his bones
down
to the river,
and as the yellow breeze
lied open
I felt the mist
of the water
scrape at my neck.

my cold
hardened
reflection
told me,
this is no dream.

I thought this morning
as the sun
crackled bright
and
frowned loud,
I should go down and see about Jacob.

maybe
I could visit him-
smell his hair
thick as the black hills,
find his eyes-
the shade of
toasted chestnuts,
touch his
lone dimple,
resting above

his right cheek.
kiss his fingers-
long
and
made for
strumming
the sounds
of southern valleys
and
northern islands.

but all I have
are his bones
in my hands.
all I have
are moments
that belonged
only to us,
and
regret
of any plan
made without him.
I have
the deep ache
that rushes
when someone is with child.
I have
the narrow chills
that follow me
on evening walks
under a howling quilt
of sheen.

by the river
I can find
some trace of him.
here,
I am with the
only person
that will ever
know me
and
here,
I am just
another stone
drowning under
moonlit water
but somehow
he feels close-

and that will have to do for now.

AIN'T IT JUST LIKE THIS WORLD TO KEEP YOU LONESOME

when you are down
for a long time
and have gone spoiled,
when the wind
catches you in the face
and is carrying voices
beyond the sea,
when the twilight hours blow
all your dreams away
and melts the sun
streaming at your chin
and turns it into the blues
as evening falls,
when living
feels like sighing
you will notice-
no company is found.

no calls will find
your ear
and
no letter will arrive
on a lonesome day.
maybe they know
I have given up
looking for you-
which makes me sink,
crawling
far
back
into the sheets.

and in the
darkest shadows
of the mighty pines
there are moments I pray
for just a familiar voice,
the strumming of strings
or
even a highway truck
that whines.
I will take a drunk
coughing up hickory
or even
a frail
and
wandering
shoulder
to lean on.

but when
boxcars groan
and western shores creep,
when the junk stops working
and you are waiting
for the ax to fall,
I wish just one person
would look me in the eyes
and say,
I would cross
the icy rivers
for to ease your pain.

but you will find no company,

you will find the
dark
punishing
the breeze.

you will hear
the barnyard call
of a wounded night.

yes,
you will find
a whole lot
of nothing.

ODE TO LITHIUM

thank you
my friend
for soothing
the highs
and
the lows,
the dark
and
the less dark,
the dreams
and
the daylight.

thank you
for making
me
just like
everyone else-
a faded star
blinking
and
hoping
endlessly
won't
last too long.

the
red skin
molded
onto my cheeks?
all
thanks

to you,
old friend.

a final
thank you
is in order
for
making
me
so much
better
than
anything
I could
ever hope
to
erase
in myself.

FREIGHT TRAIN BLUES

there is gold to be had
on the other side
but there is
sorrow
that travels
with the
freight trains
at night.
on this
lonesome railway
lined with
buttered blossoms.

the bell ringer
made you a promise-
we are here to carry the blues away
bound for glory,
you are told.

you might have a place
to fall in the morning
and a chance
to get up
by dusk,
but this rusty metal
is about the only thing
to get you to the other side.

it is somewhere between
them and me,
the snow sobs down in july
the wind

blows under
the sea
and
starlight cannot find you.

but once those rails stop
spinning their wheels,
there is gold to be had
on the other side.

as for me,
I could never
hop on the express line,
not even the scenic route.
there might be gold
on the other side
but down here
I know
the price
of selling your soul
on those diamond tracks.

and I tell those passengers
before they board,
be careful
not to let
that sunshine
fool you.

WAITING AROUND TO DIE

I pace
on a
golden morning
and tell myself
to care.

my body
steeps long
in a cup of dreams
as one day
turns
into
seven.

I whimper
as my eyes
make rain
out of sweat.

and while the
light hangs
low
and
shines raw,
while the
call of the nightjar
dismisses the day,
I notice
all I am doing
is
waiting around to die.

MY FRIEND

I would like to lean
into the sky
and tell myself I am free
but living out here,
I am hiding from
the scented mist
of evening-
feeling what this
honest world
has to give me.

watch who you love
friend,
even when
the approach of night
feels soft.
love not a world
that is made of stone,
that spits back at the sea,
and rejects the loving arms
of the morning tides.

tread lightly in her eyes
friend,
for in the daylight
you will
find yourself
standing among the ones
yes, the ones.
their wandering minds
do not find midnight,
their feet walk faster

than their thoughts,
and they have
never heard
dying words.
there is no one
left
like you,
friend.
and you cannot
seem to find
another that knows
a blue day
pouring down
is more lonesome
than any night.

but it ain't all bad,
friend.
when you
are feeling down
and
the thought
of all this living
that is left
makes you weary
take a walk to my house.
find yourself in me-
I will stand by your side,
whisper sweet words,
and together we can
find a way to hold onto
the falling rain of springtime.

A CRACK IN THE WINDOW

the night
folds its arms
across the sky
and melts the sun
behind
the hillside,
down along
small gaps
of hardened shale.

oh,
the scent of dusk-
it tails
the skirt chasers
and glints
along
the jitters
that hang.

but there is a crack
the blues
keeps
shining
in on,
rolling
with
the
sweet breath
of moonlight.

I am
tossing

and
turning
and
my back
is bruising.
my foamy eyes
are growing restless,
and my feet
are fitted
with the
drawls
of the blues.

an empty bottle
does nothing
to sooth
these empty people.

i just have to lie here.

you are a
regular
old blues.
and this
must
be my
evening
lullaby.
you force
my heart
to hammer
and mouth

to throb.

the old blues
soars with
the night howl
and howls
with the night.

please bring him back.

there is a crack
the blues
keeps shining
in on,
but only some of us
can feel it.
this old stick
brings us to
some distant time,
and even here
we are bound
to find the blues.

only a fool thinks
they can
beat the devil
around the stump,
but many will try.

and when
you tie up those
flying shoes

and patch on
the red light-
my friend,
the day you arrive
on that
golden coast
you will find
there is a crack
the blues
keeps shining in on.

WHAT COLOR DID THE MOON DANCE?

what color
did the moon dance
when you fell at my feet?
did the soft light
shimmer blue
through our window
and into my hands,
resting on yours?

did tears from
a smiling heart
splash across
our faces
as we slept?

did the wind lie deep
under our door
as we woke up
with one another?

I wonder
what it was like
when the mountains
knew
of our love,

you have been mine
for as long
as I can
ever remember
and now,
it is just me.

I have thrown myself
into
the black
of nightfall.
I do not walk
these hills lightly,
for my toes have
almost hit the ground
and
I can
barely crawl
my way back.

GOOD MORNING BLUES

my window mutes
the soft coo
of the
mourning dove,

they sure have the blues with every trill-

the dawn is
fixing to storm
like many days before
and many days to come,
but I have not heard
their song
on my cup
in some time.

I love the mourning dove,
a born carver
and a
true
artist
in their line.

but even though
they have
the blues
in their berries,
and
even though
they have
the blues
all up in their seeds,

they do not grieve
the birth of daylight
or protest
the passing of time
like me,
a crazy fool-
blowing bubbles
with the flies
and
wringing wet
with sorrow.

they simply
greet the blues
in the morning
with a

hello,
how are you?

HOUSE OF MOURNING

the hole that is left
from your loss
is very deep
and
beyond reach
from the sun.

my heart
is shackled
in a net
and
my hands
are rusted
in chains.

if the day
of one's death
is better than
the day of
one's birth,
why keep me here
in this lifeless body?
why lock me in
this house of mourning
with no pallets
left in sight.

why give me the comfort
of strangers who stare,
singing the songs
of the forgotten
with an appetite

for things
new
and old,
but mostly new.

what is left
from your loss
is very sharp,
and beyond reach
from the sun-
so please,
draw up the shades.

cut off this hot iron
and
let me loose
from the bucket.
fresh pus
is pouring
and I ain't talking right.
my mind
is like some nightcrawler
swallowing the dirt
but never
tasting its fruiting flesh.

only fools think
they own the wind,

those who know better
are in pursuit of it,

those who know best
stand in awe of it,

and because
I am broken,
I crumble before it.

WELL SHIT, LOOK AT THAT

well shit,
look at that-
salt does
cover the clouds
as the
damp curtains
turn a
sunny afternoon
into a
dusky
red night.

all I do is sit.
tears shed often
but I refuse
to be like them,
all they do is
talk
and
talk,

every moment
tirelessly
documented
and
self
promoted.
all this fanfare,
but they have not learned
how to love
their fellow man
or

their fellow woman.

I hate feeling this lonely all the time.

I had you
in my heart
for 14 years
and
on my lips
for 7.
how lucky,
to find
him so young
but to lose him,
so soon?
well shit,
look at that-
here I am.
everything
and
everyone
falling short.
all these people
wasting their
screams
and
sobs,
on what?
you may
labor long
but you have
never given birth.

I am like a boat
far from land
and all at sea,
drifting fast
with
each new hour.
I am floating
wherever
the current
drags me,
smothered
by all these
layers
and
layers
of
marshy smoke.

I am coughing
and tipping
with rocks
in my pockets
and
dirt
in my shoes.

well shit,
look at that-

I never even had both oars in the water.

ON TRINITY RIVER

wipe the sleep out
of my crying eyes
sit with me
or stand,
gaze into
these woods
as the
damp
morning
goes chasing
behind the sun.

the fog
is buttered with
a frosted wind,
hanging low
on the trinity river
and changing
real fast,
like the way
milk steams
until it froths.

just as
the dawn's light
fixes to blow
orange hues
on the forest floor,
I smell the grass
dripping off
the sacred drizzle
of the roaming stream.

I hear
the call of
yawning birds
and
I feel
a whistle
floating
on my back
like the way
sparkling springs
cling to the mountainside.

hhhhhhmmpppppphhhhh.

this is you now,

you are the sun
you are the wind
and
I came here,
to hold your hand.

FIRST MANIC EPISODE

I woke up-
had to blink twice.
my yellow walls
were golden
with flames
and the white floorboards
seemed to swell with
the face
of bulging color,
like
fresh
white snow
falling on a
hemlock stand.

I felt my skin
and thought
this is not my body, where am I?
the holes in the fan
seemed to soak into
the drenched face
of the ceiling tiles.

I must be high-
my body was
bubbling with spice,
my olive crisped
words
could
dance my tongue
into the sunlight,
my arms

could ramble
with the roasted seeds
hanging from my wrists,
the dusty walls
smelled of
clammy tangerines,
and
the sound of my voice
wore the rhythm
of the beat.

my thoughts
leaped
and
bumped
and
tore across
this small room.
I gave a theatrical sermon
with my varnished feet.
I saw drought
on the horizon
and smelled
sequence
twinkling
with
melting ice.

I have found a nightspot
to mourn.
I have found a seaboard
for the countless.

and
I am drinking
from the
purest
limestone water.

my eyes haven't seen sleep
in some time,
but this is intoxicating-

there are wheelbarrows
under my legs
and fruit juice
in my eyes.

going crazy
never felt so good.

WOUNDED SOLDIER

keep the broken
drinking in
the sharp light,
keep the dreamers
resting under my pillow,
keep the artists
awake with
a fresh dose
of falling stars.

as the
silent sky
scrapes the
swollen moon
there is a
wounded soldier
lying in the meadow,
looking up
with his hands
at the
fatal mist.

there is
a lonesome range
in his mind
that turns his tears
warmed
with blood,
into teeth
flickering red.
there is a cattle call
riding in with the fog,

and maybe
this means
that here,
the river will bend.

my wounded soldier,
you trust in what
the prophets say-
a time for birth
and
a time for death.

you hold the dirt
with your
shaking hands,
you now understand
that soon
you will become
as spotless
as the soil
beneath your back.

but in these final moments
you hear a chorus of strings
and you think to yourself,
the shaggy crest
of the kingfisher
never seemed so lyric.

you feel the sun
dripping from your toes
as the high noon

breaks away.

piano keys
march beside you,
trembling with your
weary breath.

my brother,
you have
made me weep
in the kitchen
far away.

oceans might separate us
but hearing your story
of
love
and
loss,
has followed me
today
and
tomorrow.

there is hospital whiskey
for us all here
and for you,
we have tears.

but that won't do you any good.

ODE TO A FLUTED DAWN

I see the morning light
and hear the fluting voice
of just
one eastern meadowlark-
it calls as lonesome
as the freeway,
perched high upon the fence
singing to the wind.

houses come alive
as darkened shapes
reveal themselves
with the gentle touch
of a mother's hand,
and there is a
blue layer
of mist
blowing in,
rippling
frost
on the rooftops.

today
the sun is slow to rise.
some days I think
the sun got the blues.
that dawnscape
lies low
just a little too long
and I think to myself,
the sun will be a no-show.
it might stay in bed

taking the world
off its shoulders,
a much-needed rest
from
the spinning tides.

I like to think
even the mighty sun
can sink
like a
lost ship
in chartless waters,
even the mighty sun
needs to polish
its sea legs,
carrying
away
from the rope
or
carrying
on
with a good breeze.

but there is always
some asshole,
never too far away

the sunrise is at 6:52 AM today!

and just like that-
they take all the mystery
out of life.

STATE FAIRGROUNDS

there is a carousel at dawn
that moves with
the morning heat-
it feels out of place
as the day rolls on
a mighty charge
of copper.

are you lighting up the tilt sign?
no,
I am just trying
to find jesus-
on my own
this time.

the diner is opening soon,
I can hear
the car doors.
I can smell
the first cigarette
blowing
down with the brine.

it sure is a warm morning.
the
wind
swamps the floor
with its musk.
there is a drunken clown
sucking on cabbage,
and smelling
artificial christmas trees.

this clown
has gold teeth
for the catching
and a silent song
that sets a smolder
to the finely tuned grass.

some days,
it seems
all I do
is flee
from bootleg stuff
after it has
been bottled
in a barn.

some days,
there is
a patch
of canyons
next to my
needle and spoon.

some days,
there is
a wooden cowbell
singing to a restless crowd.

but maybe
these are just
war horses,
growing wilder every day

and the people
bumping my shoulder
are just growing
more lonesome
and
even more desperate
than me.

my name feels
like it belongs
to someone else,
a former life
that matches
some forgotten dream.

I can only walk these grounds
at the break of day,
when there is
not a one
to glance
at my streaming tears.

I can talk to you
out loud
about how much
you loved
to relive
your boyhood
here-
at the state fairgrounds.

together we imagined

our children
going on their first ride,
trying on fear
for the first time.
you would whisper,
don't worry buddy.
I would never
and
I mean never-
let anything happen to you.

you would
hug tight
as you
spinned him
in silk thread.

and he would
always feel
love from us.
he would never have to doubt it,
you would be different than your father.

in your eyes
he would know
that everything he is,
is more
pure
and
sparkling
than this carousel,
growing from

the wooded fields
and
twinkling
one
too many
mornings away.

A QUICK POEM BEFORE MY PSYCHOTHERAPY APPOINTMENT

look at you,
bang-up posture
with your head
facing the crowd.
those golden tips
match
their golden roots
as you
drip long
and
blow smooth.

but even so,
I bet you
just baked
a deep sweet
potato pie.
I think someone
told her
about
that mystery,
she has that
diddie wa diddie.

look at you,
bang-up posture
even though you
must be dragged out.
sure you've been known
to bend an elbow
but just one.

you have that
madison avenue
way about you,

but as your heel
sets loose
to the wind,
those
sparkling sandals
stay down with
the floor
and the rhythmic sound
is a bit
too peppy
for me
today.

you are the type
I think
to make the scene,
dancing real close
to the edge.
on the stick?
no,
on the hook.
and a
warm applause
is due
for that alone.

your clothes and skin,

fine as cream gravy.
even I can see that
as I slouch here
roostered in the daylight.

you are not someone
to ride the river with,
but you are here
and
bound to yawn
with your
glossy
leather nails.

no real question about it,
you are run down
and beat up
like a bar of soap after
a hard day's washing.

your insides are torn apart,
and once you leave her door
you put on that delicate mask-
by hook or crook
I will seem normal today!

everyone will buy
what you are selling,
my queen.
but I would rather be
doing the mashing

than making a mash.
but what do I know?
they say I am crazy.
they say
I am cracked up
and
off the beam,

and I wish somebody
would tell me
what
diddie wa diddie means.

A RHYTHM TO THE STRUGGLE

there is a rhythm to the struggle.
there is a dance we do,
hiding our sorrows from
the people we glance at
as we use
every open hour
to make just enough
to come home
and drink the dusky
sweat away.
but there is sweetness in this sweat,
in the pacing
huddled movements
of my brothers and sisters.
I see you
working hard
for people half your age
with twice the worth.
and while your lives are full of
bruising,
you have to watch
these full mouths clatter-
a bunch of
loveless breeders
effortlessly
enjoying food
and critiquing
craft cocktails.

your eyes
squint
as the oven steams,

up down
up down
ticket after ticket.
young women
with too much money
and degrees
matched with
loquacious minors,
concentrations,
and research experience
wowza!

but it has given them
a whole lot
of
nothing.
a whole lot of sounds
ringing proud,
on this
fashionable street-

I'm literally.
preggos!
on a skinny day
I wake up like this right?
send me that video,
bitch.

these are the lonesome tunes
that fuel the struggle.
these people rule the world,
they sign our checks,

they demand attention
but do nothing to earn it.

oh my god if you post that, I would just die!

you are spitting fire, little bride.
you have not seen death.
you have not touched death.
you have not held death in your arms,
like me

how can I walk around
breathing air like grease
with a sack over my head
while they get to
roll with the blows,
not a worry in the world?

well,
they are much better
at this whole living thing.
they sure do believe
the lies
their lungs
are selling.

and you,
my hardworking brothers and sisters-
those who can turn
night into day,
those who can get their fill
when the sun shines,

those who can hang a picture
when given a bag of nails,
those who can boil coffee
when the gas runs dry,
you,
my spirited brothers and sisters
are stronger than me
and will carry on
for all of us who cannot.

A WIDOW'S WHISPER (AND I AIN'T TALKIN' ABOUT THE CALIFORNIA KIND)

when all my
bright gold
turns
slowly
to blue,
will our memories be gone?

when
the melt
in my mouth
falls from
stained glass
into
the cold wind,
will your voice
begin to fade?

when
my fountain pen
spits out
and
bows down
will our story
soak up?

please say no.

FIXIN' TO DIE

If I close my eyes,

will you be here in the morning?

my love has
plum scented cheeks
and
doves do deliver
olives to our
window
when he laughs.

my love breathes
into my mouth,
like the wind
gasps
a roaring
into a starlit valley.

my love
takes my hand and
shows me I am
wrapped in warmth.

could you kiss me once more?

let me smell your
thick brownly shining hair,
and feel your eyelashes
rest on mine.

could you take me with you?

show me
the ceiling
of your mind,
and the glisten of
your dreaming hours.
if I close my eyes,

will you be here in the morning?

as the sun melts in
above the
freely flowing leaves,
I know the answer is no.

but I ain't
feeling funny
this time
because lord,
I believe I am fixin' to die.

WHEN I FALL INTO DREAMING

when I fall
into dreaming
by time or
through force,
I see you.
I bundle up
this body
full of
gold bricks
because
I am finally
resting with you.

I hold your
maple cream hands
and float beside
your warmed flesh.
I blush when you
stroke my face
and salute
my cheeks.

when I fall
into dreaming
I walk with you
on the heels
of sweet fern
whistling high
on a right fitten kind of day.
and to our surprise,
the lemon
begins to drop

as we glide.

when I fall
into dreaming
well-
it is just
me and you
kid,
mouthing our love
as it always was,
and
should have
always been.

I laugh with you here.
we drift slowly,
throwing petals
and
collecting milk.

when I fall
into dreaming
I tickle our children
I see myself pregnant
and I smile at
the white caps
of the salted sky.

but when the
waking hour
shines in,
I have to

convince myself
none of this will ever happen.
your voice,
just a whisper from the dust
and I can only hear it
in my sleep.

I am like the hungry ones,
who eat like
a steam engine
guzzling down coal,
but wake
to find
sour rolls
with no jelly.

I am like the thirsty ones,
who dream of
strained juice
and
fruit jars
but wake
to find
a bitterly dry mouth-
unable
to
even declare
their thirst.

and
every morning
I curse

the gray dawn
for taking me
out of your arms.

aghhhhh,
look at me-
I ain't even worth
the powder to
blow me up.

JUNKIE BLUES

small dented bags
hover around
big spoons.
bent straws
stretch
and
fold
across the dashboard.

these objects decorate my dreams.

orange capped needles
lay still beside
the cotton balls
and
the napkins,
always
with
a little blood.

when the junk is deep
I walk to the store
with irish eyes.
words float from my lips
as easily
as they are
delivered to me.
I hug the woman beside me,
and I feed the cashier
with a smile.
the sun finds a way to
come out

behind the clouds,
just for a little while.

the junk is a master.
it tricks me into thinking
I could be
something better than
my blues.
I walk with moonstones
on my hips
and guzzle down
the shaken flames.

but there is always
the moment
when I sigh,

I am back to my ugly self.

back to drinking
beef tea
with the black crow
at dusk.

back to peeling
the skin from my arms,
saying goodbye
to the food
of yesterday
and hello
to the burning chills
of morning.

and then finally,
when
just one more time
turns into
the last time.

GOLD IN MY POCKET

the gold in my pocket
is no good for the using
or the melting.
ah,
my favorite dive-
the railroad blues
on west holland avenue,
this old place has been
putting out
my flames all winter.

the cracks on the floor,
they do shimmer
like burning wood
on top of the mississippi.

but flying in
through the door
the north wind
delivers me
some shining
road dust-
a shadow of something homemade,
a traveling piece of stone
with stories
of distant hills
and lovers lying alone.

cold nights
with warm liquor
is the only way I can
lock any of you

between those
blue moons rising.
but that is some mighty fine
road dust you got,
and
everyone
knows
I have been
waiting
for it
all season.

I can hear music
fading into night
hmmm,
my fragile body might
just make it out of here alive.
I am on the crust
of this place
or maybe
I am
just in protest
of daybreak,
but I am going
to hitch a ride
with some of that dust.
get myself
floating to another city
or smoking over
new pockets of ocean
or maybe just settling
underneath

a field of
yellow blooms
but
I am going

I am gone.

I LOVE THE SMOKER

I am grateful I am not you.
I do not
fill my heart
with
plastic dreams
and
my head with
so much,
of
so little.

I see my faults
and always have-
black holes clinging
to my nose
like the way
the seeds
of
strawberries
hang
onto
fat skin,
wax dripping
from my ears,
hair growing
fast from my toes,
too sensitive to breathe
and
too repulsed to sigh.
full of love
for a memory
and only at peace

while sleeping.

yes
I see my faults
and always have
but I must say,
I love the smoker.

I am grateful I am not you,
coughing at the sight
of a lone cigarette's trail.
your eyes catch
the smoker
in disgust
as you
cover up
your mouth
and
wave the wind
in front
of your
face.

I am grateful I am not you,
holding steady
to the
park bench
because
the smoker has
come to share
some of your sun.

yes
my faults are many
and my breath is bad
but I am grateful
I am not you.

your type-
always the first to ask,
how did they die?
instead of
how did they live?
easily impressed
by
gold names
and
big words.

always the first to say,
I understand
instead of
tell me how?
you talk
over many
but
of course,
listen poor.

any moment
that your mind
could rest,
you flood it up.
well,

it don't take a genius
to spot a goat
in a flock of sheep.

I am grateful I am not you,
you get angry often
you blame others
you numb yourself
usually with
new pillows,
new clothes,
or a…
succulent garden
placed
near your
kitchen window
and
below
the
rustic
coffee canister.

you call the homeless
bums
and
the mentally ill
useless junkies,

I am grateful I am not hooked
on your junk.
it is true
I have lost fear

of the needle,
but at least
I am not
chasing it
with a straw
like you.

DEATH IS NOT STRONGER THAN LOVE

death is not strong enough
to take away
the scent of grape on your lips,
the almond shape of your eyes,
the way you wrapped your legs
around mine,
and
how
only you
could make me shine
like the way
blossoms of the spring
come open for the sun.

death is not strong enough
to take away
the way
of your arms,
wrapping my skin
with your mist
like some
freshly fallen
rainwater.

your light kisses
floated on my neck,
smothered me
in pollen,
and
always found
secret corners of my flesh.

death is not strong enough
to take away
how your tongue met mine,
how our lips trailed one another,
and
how your wet hair
rested on my thumbs
as we raced to become one.

you fed my woven wire.

your laugh made
the moonlight shine dull
and
as I slept a sounding,
you whispered
in my ears
I love you, sweet girl
I hope this is getting in there.

It felt so good when you
looked at me
sweating-
your breath
singing
endless devotion.

your moans fluttered
like the calls
of a
wood thrush
at dawn.

death is not strong enough
to take away
your warmth,
like
buttermilk
and
balsam
flowing
inside me.

I AM GOING TO RISE THIS MORNING

I am going to rise
this morning,
I believe I will shake
the dust from my feet.

I am going to rise
this morning,
I believe I will sweep
the fire down my throat.

I am going to rise
this morning,
I believe I will drink
the boiled grinds in my cup.

I am going to
rise this morning,

and that is enough.

ROAD TO NOWHERE

the road to wilderness
is not the safe road
or the selfish road,
it is not a guided road
led by clouds
in the day
and lit by fire
at night,
it is a path facing the sea
but never feeling the water
or chasing the tides-
it is the edge of the wild here.

some salty wind
might hit my face
but I,
like many before me
find myself
in the land of confusion.

the twilight hours
make me desperate,
wishing for a sign-
something
anything.

I have found myself
on this road
because
I refuse
to be another
rider in the red sea,

blind or
pretending to be
but really,
which is better?

there is no way
for me to be like them,
saving their living
for another day
and ignoring the
midnight struggle
of the mind.

it may seem
I have given up
out here
on the road
to wilderness,
but I am
just
trying
to hang on.

THE CALL OF THE BARN SWALLOW

on north san angelo street
just beyond
the wooden floors
of jo's bar,
I hear the call
of barn swallows.

only but a few
fly high
in the country air,
making mud cups
above this lodge.

but I guess this means
the snow is bound to melt,
and the spring light
is just days away.
when those blue feathers
line the doors
I rub my neck,
time
is
almost out.

I have been
living in this room
for
months
and
months,
the winter air
is an excuse

to drink all day,
walk these
dirt roads at night,
chase my tears
with cigarettes,
and follow
the lonely
path
to the grave.

I have been hiding out
since it all happened,
and it seems
my feet
are jumping
from
grass
to
grain.

but once the frost
dries out,
I cannot hide
with the blues any longer.
I take on a new name,
a new face

go see my mother and father.

it always takes
these swallows
to bring me back home.

ODE TO WELTSCHMERZ

when your warmth
is still in our bed
but your body is
lying cold
beneath my arms,
it seems the weariness
of the wind
will never stop.

it is a whistle
that brings about
the flies.
it is a steep ravine
sloped high from my feet
with blooming dogwood
shaking on top.

the scent of howling wine
drips like syrup
on my mouth,
like when your
tongue roamed
between my legs.

I got a hellhound on my trail-

and when you forget
to reject the bad
or praise the good
well,
what do you have left?

there is an endless shame
in my desire to be squashed,
to remain nameless
and drift often-
resting with the gamblers
and sitting among the drunks.

my sorrow in these moments
is never loud enough
to tell the world
about the metal
drilled into my bones.
the sweat bubbling
from my chin
is never drained
by those
I silently weep for.

there is a desert sun in us all,

and your lid might lift
but nothing will stick.

this life
seems to be
the seasonal tilling
of the land.

row
by
row
these rooted plants

turn into mounds of dirt,
some get to flower
for another year
or two
but even
old trees
must wither-
stranded
and
without love.

THE CRAFTSMAN THAT CARVES

to you,
I say
thank you
for believing
in magic.

you see
wood
and whisper: *wake up!*

you carve
life into the fingers
of knotty pine
and
muted stone.

you make
seabirds and queens,
villages
and
ruby grained homes-
you
breathe life
into
the
lifeless.

thank you,
my friend.
you got the only
crown of thorns
worth selling.

MY LOVE

my love
fell pure as the snow-
he drank freely
in open waters
and fed
the sparkling pools
of delta mist
with his smile.

my love
danced with
his rolling feet
and laughed with
the chilling tides
of life.
he walked
for me
through me
and
with me.

my love
how he loved…
in all the world,
not a love like mine.
he kissed me ripe
and held on purring-
always to be found
whenever I called.
and no matter
how wet
his eyes fell

he could always
shed more tears
for me.

my love
swam the seas
to hear me laugh,
he saw flowers
in my teeth
and whistling bells
of scarlet
on my hair.

and when the sun
greased our sheets
while he lied
lonesome
or came down
with thoughts
running faster
than his breath-
he would
always
listen to me
talk about
my dreams first.

my love
was the day
that lies open.
he was
a frozen lake

for my tasting,
a field of daisies
for my sucking,
and
an open dirt road-
winding along
with the
restless skies
of dusk.

my love
never wandered
to another
in flesh
or in
storm.

his love for me
was fed
with
each
new moon.

he looked at me
naked
and
flawed
and said
you are perfect,
may our souls
stay forever
locked in time.

my love
was the
sailing ships
along morning.
he was the clouds
above
on a summer day.
he was the calm
that settles you
when you
fall awake
whispering
to the door.

my love
knew
my suffering
and I knew his.
he felt this world
like me.
he sang my praises
to anyone with
an ear
to beg
or
borrow.

we promised
each other,
each other
for always.

and now
I am raw,
so lost
and
so broken
because
you
my love,
are gone.

the blues is falling down like hail.

I never
got to kiss
those
beautiful lips,
like buttered sugar
or
smell your skin,
like dripping melon

I never got to
dream with you
or do
so much of
what I love to do
with you,

one last time.

my love
are you here?

yes
that is you.
you are right behind me,
stirring my drink
and
bulging at my neck.

but I can
only find you
in the
quiet hours
of sweat,
when
the drugs have
all worn off
and
I can
feel myself
going insane.

LOST ON METROPOLE AVENUE

it is plain to see
the sun ain't shining
on winter's clock.

my love lies
underneath my feet,
climbing
with the wind
and resting on
the soul of
a broken night.

these crawling hours
polish my blood
as
the days
bend slow.

I stare at the ceiling
sleeping,
turning,
wishing for
something
to burn out,
faces to become his

but the voices all
sound hollow
with nothing to serve.

I can feel him.
he is all around me,

sifting gold from
flying clouds.
he is laughing for me
when I am weak
and crying with me
when I am
kneeling
in gloom.

but the loneliest breaths
are the ones
where he is lost,
not a trace
of his cloth
to save me from
the scorching heat

no shadow
of his hand
when the
high waters
come surging,

but I know his feet walk here.

I have to remember
his steps drain
with mine,
wherever I go.

but I want
his hand

on mine
not
a shadow
in the sky
or
blinking
of the sun.

WILD WATER

sip on me
wild water
of the rocky shoals.

spiced grapes,
with your
sweet milk
and hair
hanging long,
be gentle
with my body
as it flows
down your river.

above me,
onion blades
ring faint
like a
bell tower
floating by
undiscovered
and
surrounded
by mountain ash,
like
the chapel
of transfiguration.

busted hills
on the snake river
glisten and kink
but my eyes

will never see
the morning sun
upon the
mud's breath.

the fire
colored
poplars
shake the grate
as I swim,

but their coats of red
will never warm me
like they once did.

nature went
from sacred
to something
I shrug at.

I spent hours
and hours
staring at
the wildflowers
of my youth.
but now,
I see them as…
well,
I don't even see them.

I don't miss them, either.

my loss has taken it all-
it has silenced
the sand
drifting
like seaweed,
darkened
and
nearly cut dead
beside a
cherry laurel.

alone and forsaken
by fate
and
by man,

left with
the songs
of the trailing winds
and
the wheezing call
of this
wild water.

THE LAMB IS WORTHY

the pines shiver
below the stars
like the way
dusty glitter
falls lonely
on twilight.

my mind
is hammering
at my teeth,
and as
white
sprinkled moons
rest by my feet,
I could never forget
that spring
only
blooms
from his
lips.

it all means nothing.

there is a
constant parch
of
the daylight hours.

the lamb is worthy
but
I am not.

the prayers
of the saints
do me
no good,
not sure
they ever did.

but the oil
wine
and
barley
mix well
with the
fire
burning down
my veins.

there is nothing
in me
to chant for
to rise for
to cheer for

no spirit to awaken-

just
a whole lot
of digging
underground
with my hair
railed
below

the sand,
flying
far from me
and
far from
that sacred
oak,

our oak.

ON FAITH

his army is gone,
swimming in the sea
and drowning
under the flames.

but the way I see it,
redemption
was brewed
strong for them,
and left nothing
but water for me.

clear and without
sugar,
clear and without
scent,
something you need
but never what
you crave.

you gave
them words
from
a high mountain
near saint catherine
and me?
just an old dirt road
dusty and
endless,
with flowers
shedding off
their skin.

keeping me alive?

wrapping me
loose in pain?

no child left
to hold my hand?

well,
you can praise
whatever you want-
but
I call that
a golden calf.

I TRIED TO LIVE FOR A ROSE POGONIA

there is no more
sour mash
around here.
goddammit-
I am drunk again
and forgot to
take the
sweet salt
that makes
my brain
stop whispering
voices
to my head.

maybe I will take a walk.

the piney hills unfold
a wet and
smiling
rose pogonia.

the best kept
secret of this
old river bed
lie just northwest
of pine bluff.

the longest bayou
in the world
is here,
and the
swampy waters

cut up the air
with the
steamy broth
of southern
summers.

I can barely walk
half a mile
without collapsing
under the shade
of a willow oak.
this place is
well within
the floodplain,
but well outside
the arms of
development.

the spoonbills are
humming with
the winter
and
the winter
hummingbirds
are busy
getting full
off seaside nectar.

I have seen enough.

there is a part of me
that dies

with each breath
and a part of me
that thinks even this
rose pogonia
is worth sticking around for.
but the wolves are bound
to chase the moon away,
the sheep will eat up
all the branches,
and I guess
someone has to lick the ice.

I cannot shake his loss
with the tumbling down
of my body.

the mountains,
my bones
and the rocks,
my teeth.
the rivers,
my blood
and the rays of sun,
my hair.
everything is coming down.

found my pills.

I wish
this field of
pastel pink could do it,
how I pray

this twinkling orchid
could be enough.
it has swimming feet
and delights
in the arms
of the afternoon.

but your swaying
will not help me
and
your tupelo scent
must be left
to drift on
someone else.

if there is an ear listening,
could you cut the night in half
and tie the clouds into a bow?

could you do something
to make me believe in you
or give me
some kind of…

ahhhhhh.
I can feel them kicking in.

good night.

WALK ACROSS THE PLAINS

flakes of the herd
have been driven
from this land
to the one
behind me.

no matter where
you ramble
or end up sorting yourself,
on good farming lands
or on the west side
of some
well groomed
village-
none of that really matters,

everyone
is bound
for the
long
walk
down.

the walk
across the plains
seems to be
the only thing
we all
share.

not
one man

or
one woman
has lived a life,
and not had to
march
the
lonesome trail
under the
cruel shine
of the sun.

there is no getting out
alive
my friends-
this land
is fenced in
and the
white topped
wagons
make sure
you stay
on path
and
on time.

soon
the drizzle
of light
from
windows of far-off towns
will shed
their glow,

one
by
one.

but you have plenty
of walking time
to remember
how you loved
what you lost
how you always
pushed westward
and did just as best
you could.

when you get
to the end of the line,
you will not
be able
to spell
your name,
you might start
howling at the moon
or in anger,
shoot fire
at the forgotten
county road.

but when the plains
begin to
crumble up into
mountain slopes-
you will

shed just one tear
and remember
all you did.

and even though
there might be a
mother road
waiting for you,
you make peace
with the rutted ditch
you are likely bound for.
and this
is when
my stranger on the plains,
we all
share
just
one soul.

and I will
always feel you,
like the way
night
holds
onto winter,

like the way
morning
funnels
into spring,

and like the way

these
plains
smolder blindly
into
the smoky hills.

ALONG THE RAILROAD

you speak
to my
streaming
moonshine,
sweet boy.

the cast iron sky
follows
the tears I have
been choking down
and
shaking out.

I have made my bed,
chased my elbow
to get to my thumb,
and
sold damn near
all my clothes.

I shut my eyes today
and once again
saw your body
lying
lifeless,
as the young
men
drip sweat
and
push down
trying
to make

you gasp
or beat.
I cannot live
with these images
anymore,

my family is gone-

and all I have left
are moments
so violent
I feel
like I am being
whispered
to my
grave.

I am told
you must
dream of the heavens
before you
unlock the gate,

swim on the peak
before you
limp uphill,

taste the glow
before you
pull back the blinds,

stand under red clouds

before you
bask in the sun.

but I also
know
you must
lose yourself
in
yourself.
find a
golden hour
laced with
happiness
or even
a stable mood
will do.

but still dream,

for all of us
who lost
the singing harps
beside
our pillows.

please keep the spark
sacred,

for
the desperate
and
picked off,

for those of us
blind pigs,
doing time
out here
on the
broken-down line.

PECAN CREEK

losing my mind
on pecan creek
seems like
a good way
to waste an hour
or two.

these people
around here
never seen my face
and I better keep it that way.

downslope from my feet,
broken rocks
keep falling
deeper and
wider
than any
midnight canyon
lighting up
the sky.

spring fed rivers
rush
and
drizzle down
along
pebbly stones.

here,
the wind
is cool

and
the red sand
mixes with
clear water
and
ashy clay.

there is
space
to be had out here,
and after a while
I can go back to town
start looking for
some help,

you lost your marbles again,
at pecan creek you say?

well yes,
I am always losing
those darn things down there.

GO TO WAR

I have not
gone
to war
yet
not thinking
myself
fit
for all
its hardships.

how can I
face anyone
with this
wide pair
of
blistered feet?

just like the way
hot air
smokes
up
and
over
some heated pool,
all the fog
left inside me
is searching for
some breath
in the night sky,
something
to drill
into the ice.

I have not gone
to war
yet
because I
am turning
with the wind,
like a pack of kites
tightly dancing
across the sky
but this time
my lines
are getting
turnstyled
with the
winter storm.

even though
the muted shades
of petals
gust and
glint
from warm to cold,
I know
my lungs
are full
of tar.

I weep
away
the harvest moon
with some
curled up

sun
sprinkled
on my chest.

clouds bathe
with the glow
of dawn,
but I can
still hear
what
the dust
is telling me,

oh my dear.
do not
go
to war
just yet
for
you are
not
fit
for all
its hardships.

GOLDEN NIGHT

as I awoke,
the hills turned
into sheep
and ran away
with the flock
of a golden night.

the mountains
sunk
like stones,
once skipped
beyond
a forgotten
memory.

and
as I walk,
I get junk piled.
and
as I walk,
I get
tangled
in the strings
of an
old ghost net.

my life is
down in the dust
and
my lips are weary
with grief-
but surely

someone
has to keep
their word?
my foot
is bound
to slip
and the liquid fuel
I got is
no good-
my heart
feels like
dripping
sludge
on some
drifting
current.

it all feels different,
like I am
being swallowed up
by the noon.
and as I turn around
the river breaks
into rapids
and the
jewels of summer
fold into
cream.

but nothing
will ever feel
right again.

there is nothing
to calm my tears
or lift my hopes
but him-
and he is
dead
forever,
and
ever.

oh how I wish
I could hide
on the eastern horizon
or settle under
the western limits
but,

there is no hiding from this.

I REALLY WANT TO KNOW

aw,
there are so many craft breweries here!

listen,
whatever gets you through the day
I'm on board.
for what gets me,
almost has me gone.

but for a moment
can we just be honest
my friend.
why do you like these places?
tell me,
I really want to know.

is it the young
starry-eyed girls
in nursing school,
or
all the men
dressed like
a farmland
threw up
on some vacant lot,
as they celebrate
the end
of law school?

is it all the
four-flushers
behind the bar

that make you feel
like your money
is unwanted,
your presence
too much to bare?

is it the board games
on the shelf
that you and everyone else
will remark,
how cool that is!

is it the dim lighting
that makes you forget
how much you are paying,
is it the orange
and
blackberry
amber ale
with notes
of oak,
that has been
brewed
just for you
and your manicured hands?

people my age
flock to these places
like a cactus wren
takes to
yucca.

I heard on the news,
some old miserable fucker
say,

elitism,
or something else?
millennials and the war on big beer...
most people,
not just
my
dreadful
clan,
think they are better than
everyone else.
come on
even you know that.

it seems what's going on here
is pretty simple.
filter is
praised
at any cost,
and the
homespun
disposition
is winning out.

they say
I was born in the wrong decade
but the problem is
they are
are very much

of their time,
they share photos of
wild west saloons
or ghost towns
off route 66
with their tits hanging out
and
their shimmering shoes
crossed out and blurred.

for me,
I will always breathe
too close
to the night
to ever care
what brand
of cigarettes
I buy
or
what percentage
of corn is in my
whiskey
or
how local
the wine is
or
how farm to table
the restaurant is,

any of that stuff
that just
drips

and
bakes
smoke
and
mirrors.

but like I said before,
whatever gets you through the day
I'm on board.
for what gets me,
almost has me gone.

LOONY BIN LOVE SONG

to the one
who spills out
the fourth bowl,
if you are
listening-
pour down on me.

I heard they gave
you one of the best,
your bowl
will take
the heat
from
the sun
and smother
us all
with smoke-
scorched
with
brimstone,
I heard them say.

the seventh bowl seems
too risky,
that
hundred
pound
hail
might not
land
down here
in the flats.

and the first bowl?
well,
you have to swim
in the sea
to taste the blood.

my money is on
number four-
drowning
in smoke
seems much better
than
choking
on
some
gnawed tongue.

let me see a few
other bowls
before you come get me.
I want to see
ripe islands
flee into
the lonesome ocean.
I want to hear
the drunken slurs
of that woman
who drank
up st. peter,
before
they leave her
flat busted

and
on the dole.

throw
petals on my head
and
send me
in line
with the seafarers
and the shipmasters.

show me just
one magic trick
because,
the fruit I crave
has left me,
the milk I nurse
has run dry,
the wine I bottle
has gone sour,
and
the spice box
of earth
has lost
all its flavor.

ME AND THE DEVIL

take me down
an old wagon road
and settle me
deep in the far west,

there is rambling
on my lips
and without my baby here
I might as well
leave this morning
and head to the
paradise
river
valley.

nothing to lose
except my mind,
but that happens
just about
everywhere.

I am bound to
trade stories
with
the great grandsons
of mountain traders
and fur trappers.

there is something
that brings me back
to
hmm…

I guess
wanting to live,
when I
watch my feet
circle above
the rocky whites
and
channel catfish.

out here
the people seem
to frolic,
they fire
at glass bottles
and dance with
the breaking of leaves.

I am not like them,
smiling
from one horizon to
the next.
I am not like them,
spirits as high
as the hills
their children
glide.

I am a
shaggy monster.

I am a
broken-down train.

I am rusty metal
in the middle of
a spring blooming
meadow.

I am not like them,
they roam
like some far off herd
and in the winter months
these people
huddle together,
bonded
in their warmth
as they share
smoking pipes.

I am not like them
because they have
a family
to offer blankets
in the
season of light.

fuck-
I am so broken,
like a
blazing log
camped under
a blizzard.

I am the grass
that is

marched on
in circles
and
in piles.

I am like the
desperate hunter
who kills a bison,
scrapes out his
pulpy flesh
and crawls into
the empty carcass
to escape
a frosted night,
but in the morning
I wake up
to find
myself a prisoner-
the mighty ribs
have frozen together
above me.
I am locked
in tightly
and
because
I am alone,
no one will come
looking for me.

no need to keep
one eye open
anymore,

what is the point?
I am a clump of scrub
with splinters
on my teeth.

I am filled with bullet wounds
but none of them
seem to finish the job.

I am not like them,
my hands fall into the wind.

I can see the game
they are after
but
no reason
to run
or even
watch.

I keep reminding myself
with a prayer
a groan
and
hours of tears,
there is rambling
on my lips
and without my baby here
I might as well
leave this morning.

SOUTHERN TRAIN GOT MY LUNGS

look at that train,
linking around
the old iron bridge
that rises
high above
the chattahoochee river.

it takes shape
into the forest
and
soon
disappears
like the way
the queens of the sky
fade into
a summer afternoon.

sad,
when that great ship
went down
but I am
old
and
unknown,
and my loaded feet
just want to shimmer off.

what becomes
of someone like me?
do I keep
rolling on
like some

mighty good road,
or do I give up
trying to
overcome,

find a way
for my lumpy skin
to make gold
for panning,
mud
for layering,
and
air
for breathing?

even when
the northern flicker
lights up
a lonesome night,
I still feel
hopeless,

like an
old growth forest
sold for timber,
each towering pine
destined for
the pulp mill.

like a footpath
kept up
by

a hundred years
of
daughters
laughing,
only to have
a handshake
tear it all away.

the scabs you feel
when you have
lost it all
and there is no
making sense
of the
soon
or
the
someday.

there is only now,
black steam
above the
sunflowers
and
a tip of the hat
to the
southern train
that got my lungs.

DIRTBAG CHARMER

the canned heat
is sinking low,
a few more
days
and this
dirtbag
charmer
will be
on her way.

on my way
to the battered stools
of home
where the chalk
behind the third stall
always reads,

find what you love and let it kill you.

I never knew
words sprayed
when I was
sixteen
could soak
up my skin,

like some
wet lips
on
a hunter
before
old betsy

goes down.

it tells the
story
of the
last
ten years
so
well.

but
after I chew the rag
I remember,

my grief
is doing all
but keeping
me standing,
like the
way the booze
in this place
does all
but heal you.

THE MORNING SUN

every day
the morning sun
goes down
at noon
but today,
I got hot coals
on my feet
and
my insides
are all turned up
like rocks
after a plow
breaks up
the soil.

I felt you
today,
I think.
shit
maybe I am going crazy.
but still,
I thought
your hand was
on my shoulder,
and no matter
how I walked
I could not
stumble.
it had to be you,
right?
the wind
was dripping

warm with honey
and it seemed like
I could finally
embrace
the fire
without
getting burned.
it had to be you,
right?
no,
I guess not.

but it sure felt like it.

BLACKBIRD BLUES

the eyes of dawn
got me
sipping the blues.

how can I be here again?

maple and milk
under my tongue,
drenched
in the white frost
of my dreams.

well,
I know
I was sleeping
but at least
my heart was awake.

I am a goner

here I am,
same spot
as yesterday
and
same spot
as tomorrow.

the fat
on my drums
washes down
with
blood

from
muddy creeks.

no morning star
shines
on my doorstep,
for the
blackbirds
keep
bringing in
the
high west midnight,
throwing
dry wood
on the
bitter flames
and
making sure
my
festering sores
keep rising.

EVERYTHING IS JUST ABOUT THE SAME

the wind is no warmer
the road is no shorter
and the pain is no lesser

everything
is just about the same.

the stars are
just as sharp
as they dangle
with the black mist.

the dirty grease
of sunset
is just as piping.

the flowers
I left for him
are still sleeping
on the ground
and
just as
rotted out.

the broken radio
is still buzzing
and
the empty bottles
still lie unswept,
since sometime
last month
I think.

yes,
the swelling
of my left ankle
is just as far
from me
as his dying breath
in my mouth.

you got news for me?
well,
I got nothing for you.

so
please
don't go
selling me your blues,

because
the wind is no warmer
the road is no shorter
and the pain is no lesser

everything
is just about the same.

SPRINKLE ME

sprinkle me
a sack of gold
and rub me down
with morning rays,
while the sweats
drench my
every breath
I wonder
how blue
this world can
make me.

the moon
is hiding
behind
a starless valley,

I see you over there-

she never knows
how to cool
the vengeance
in my flames,
she never knows
how to awaken
the dead hours
of my night,
she never knows
how to shield
me from
the salted gloss
of the sea,

but she must know
I am waiting
for her
to give me some news
like the way
the skipper's wife
watches for tidings
on the shore.

do not shut
your eyes,
my sleeping sun.
for I have
old stones
in my aching teeth
and
I am waiting
for
just
one
answered prayer.

I WILL BE

the wind,
the wind is blowing
through
memories of
his tidal kiss.

his lust would
drip
down
my scabbed back.

his tongue
was like
some golden syrup,
it melted my lips
with a molten spine.

his spit
held onto the
soaking pores
that
freckled my
throat.

his hands
felt like an oily brush.
he would
dig
and
dip
my juice
with his fingers.

I remember
the light
when he would
wash his mouth
in my
velvet smoke.

I remember
the spark
when
he
and only he
peeled off
my
every
ache
and
glazed
my teeth
with
his salty flesh.

I remember that
he never
forgot to,

beat the butter in a large bowl until creamy.

MIDNIGHT GLITTER

the cold snap
of march
bathes
my
jerking legs
and
goes scalding
the corners
of our
soaking sheets.

the morning
simmers
away
all the frost
at my door
and
leaves me
with
a mighty summit to climb,

but
there is
ashfall in
the far slopes
and
my weak bones
cannot fly.

I wish I could run with the springers,

but the smoking glow

from the brewing rain
beats me down
and
back down.

this life is cruel
no two ways
about it,
and the
hook
under my hair
will be growling
in my stomach
as
starlight
sets in.

I have fallen
and there is
nothing to hold,
and soon
the
broken pieces
of dusk
will
boil
off my skin
and
even that
midnight glitter
will be blinding.

WASTE OF SPACE

good morning,

aghhhhhhhhh.

my hair
is filled
with rat droppings
and
my teeth
smell
like spoiled cabbage,

unwashed
clothes
cling
to my
larded
thighs
and
curdled
cheeks,

stale dust
pours
from
my tears
and
stains
my lips.

I am disgusting.

I am
sour milk
on top
of
rancid cheese.

I am
a stairwell
mopped
with urine.

I am
the wind
of sulfur
mornings
like
hot sweat
on a graveyard,

and
I wish someone
would
just
put me
out of my misery,

I am
a
waste
of
space-

BE CAREFUL

be careful
how you run
when you
try to
make up
for lost time.

be careful
how you mourn
when you
try to
smile away
those tears.

be careful
how you hide
when you
try to
chase off
the
blues.

there are
hundreds
of bridges
bound for
the end of the line,
but none
roll in
on time
and
few will

change
direction-
even when you
try to
walk straight,
even when
someone new
comes along
to cool
your
breathing.

sometimes
when you are right
the lowlands get flooded,
and when you are wrong?
well,
the river
just
grows
smaller.

but you can always
wander into town,
find something
to ease your mind,
and come away
with your cares
in hand
and dreams
far behind you.

WHEN YOU ARE BROKEN, THE GIFTS KEEP COMING

there was
a time
I once thought,
these clouds
would never
return
after
the rain.

I had melted
under
the blue moon
and surely
nothing more
would
pour down
from the
surface
of the
wind.

give it some time,

clouds
always
come back,

just like
the turning
of day
or the

draining
of pus,

there is
always
more
once you
get that
shaking
hand
steady.

RIDER ON A WHITE HORSE

at the top of the hill
there is a rider
on a white horse,
his robe is soaked
in blood
and
he shines
just like an angel
in the flesh
of the sun.

but then I see my
face,
bubbling
like a
sweaty hog
waxed
with
crooked oil
and
thick mud.

you are an ugly piece of shit.

it feels like
the sea
is spitting up
all the dead
inside me.

if there is a key
that gets you into

the grit,
I must be next.
I feel so
low down
and
picked off
I am making
the
old prairies
look like
rolling rocks.

what happens
when your
sweet
morning star
flames out?
I think this.

I think this.

THE SKY IS NOT GLOWING

the sky
is not glowing-
it is
moaning
with a thump,
it is
hissing with
the breath
of golden fruit,
and bleeding
a pale tint
of peach,

is this you?
yes.
is this from you?
I ain't sure.
I wish.
I hope.

my feet
circle without spirit,
my legs
ramble without joy,
and the wind
cutting up
my sobs
is heard by
no one.

then
I catch

some
toughed up
busker
hum,
the sky is glowing.

no.
the sky
is not glowing-
it is
coughing
smoke
on a bending rail,
it is
dancing
on the carpet
of
diamond whiskers,
and
folding
orange light
on the
baking
shards
of grass,

is this you?
yes.
is this from you?
I ain't sure.
I wish.
I hope.

PUMPED DRY

I am pumped
dry
down
to the bones
with no end
in sight.

my skin
might
look
rosy
and
nourished
but I
assure you,
that is
just
the booze talking.

grief
has
hit me
like
a small room
with
too many
lilies,
the scent
knocks
me down
and
keeps me faint.

I am covered
in
flies
and
smothered
in
the
dead oil
from
last week's
fish.

I twitch
and
jerk
all
night long.

my sorrow
washes
over me
like
a
seasonal pond,
sometimes
the water
is only bound
to
wet my
socks,
but
hours later

I am
up to my waist
in the
mud
and
rain.

this is how
life is,
now.

this is how
I breathe,
now.

this is the cold sun,

and
I sure
ain't
sure
why
I even
bother
getting up.

thank you